The Crossing

Michael's Story

Michelle O'Connell

Published in 2016 by BMS Books
An imprint of Business Media Services Limited
5 High Street, Rotorua 3010, New Zealand
P.O. Box 6215, Whakarewarewa, Rotorua, 3043, New Zealand
Tel: 64-7-349 4107
Email: ms@bms.co.nz
URL: www.bms.co.nz
All rights reserved.
First published as The Crossing
ISBN: 978-0-473-34394-1
Second publishing as The Crossing - Michael's Story
978-0-473-35533-3
Copyright 2016 Michelle O'Connell

This book is sold subject to conditions that it shall not be lent, sold, hired out or circulated without the publisher's prior consent.

For Michael and Christopher
to remember our history
for Albert

It is dark when Mum gets ready for The Crossing. I want to go too.
'Go back to sleep,' says Mum. 'I will be home soon.'

Mum is marching all the way over the Rimutaka Hills tonight.

There will be people dressed up like World War One soldiers, real army soldiers and two hundred people will march behind them, just like Mum.

They are walking to remember the soldiers who marched over the Rimutaka Hills 100 years ago.

Mum is marching to remember my great, great grandfather Albert Turley.

When the first soldiers marched in 1915, they walked for three days…

…and camped for two nights. It was the last part of their soldier training in New Zealand.

They were now ready to go to fight in World War One in places like France and Belgium.

When Mum gets to Camp Road, everyone will be waiting to start.

At three o'clock in the morning, Mum will walk with hundreds of people to the war memorial in Featherston.

Then the big walk will start. They will climb all the way up to the top of the Rimutaka Hills in the dark and reach the Summit just as the sun is coming up.

Everyone will have breakfast together…

…just like the soldiers did 100 years ago.

It will be the first time they see the new memorial to the soldiers.

Mum promised to take me to see it soon.

I am sad when Mum leaves. I wonder if baby Ina was sad when her dad Albert left for war.

I go back to sleep...

...and dream I am a World War One soldier marching with Albert....

We march around the hills like a giant snake…

…and sail away in ships…

...to the other side of the world.

I wonder how many soldiers did not come home again.

In the morning, I look for Mum, but she is still gone.
I worry because I know she is far away.

'Is Mum coming back?'
Dad tells me Mum is walking down the Rimutaka Hills now.

The rain drips on the window and I think of Mum walking down the hills. I wonder if it is raining there too.

I get out my pens and draw me and Albert marching on the hills and sailing on big ships.

I make a surprise picture for Mum, a red soldier poppy for Albert Turley, just like the poppies she likes to paint.

Dad says Mum will be marching in the parade in Upper Hutt now, just like the parade Christopher marched in with Mum.

They are marching to the war memorial in Upper Hutt.

I think of all the people waving at the soldiers. I wish I was in the parade too.

At lunch time, Mum marches to the old soldier camp in Trentham.
I hope Mum will be home soon. She has been gone a long time.

I wait and I wait until Mum is home at last.

We snuggle up by the fire and Mum tells me all about her walk and the new soldier memorial on the Summit. I want to go and see it now, but we have to wait until we drive over the Rimutaka Hills next.

Finally, we drive to Wellington. We go around and around the giant hills.
Did you really walk all this way? I ask Mum.

When we reach the top, I see the memorial. It looks like real soldiers marching up a hill.

The wind blows and I have to hold on tight to my poppy. I put my poppy for my great, great grandfather Albert by the memorial and cover it with stones so it doesn't blow away.

And we remember Albert Turley.

We remember all the New Zealand soldiers who marched and went to World War One for us.

The Crossing Reenactment

In September 1915, the first troops left the Featherston Military Camp and marched 34 kilometres over the Rimutaka Hills to Trentham Military Camp. It was the last stage of their soldier training in New Zealand before they embarked for World War One.

They left at night in a large contingent of around 1000-2000 and walked for three days, bivouacking at Kaitoke and Upper Hutt. On their first day, the Wairarapa Patriotic Association greeted the soldiers with food and drink at the Summit. The road was little more than a dirt track and they marched in all weather. From Trentham, they travelled by train to Wellington where they boarded ships to Eygpt and then they were deployed in the Western Front.

My great grandfather Albert Ernest Turley marched The Crossing in January 1918. He left with the 34th Regiment, Company D. He departed New Zealand on the HMNZ101, 2nd March 1918, leaving behind his wife Mary and one-year-old daughter Ina. He was conscripted and had to go. Albert was at war briefly in Egypt and then went on to Brocton Military Camp, England. Like thousands of soldiers, he was affected by illness. In 1919, he was on the seriously ill list for influenza. Fortunately for my family he survived as my grandfather was born after the war.

Sadly, for many of the 30,000 who marched, the Rimutaka March comprised their last footsteps in their homeland. Of the nearly 100,000 people who served from New Zealand in WW1, around 18 000 died, their family lines ended in graves. Approximately 40,000 more were wounded or suffered illness. Had Albert suffered the same fate, none of my family would be here now.

On September 27th 2015, 100 years after the first march, Tweet Bird and The Reenactment Committee organised the reenactment of The Crossing. 250 people left Camp Road, Featherston, Wairarapa at 3 am and marched more than 23 kilometres to Kaitoke, Wellington, then travelled by bus to Davis Field, Trentham. Police, ex-servicemen, and civilians marched in replica World War One uniforms and hobnail boots at the head of the march, followed by Linton Camp army personnel in full combat gear, army cadets and around 200 descendants of the original marchers. Wreaths were laid at the Featherston and Upper Hutt memorials. The Rimutaka Summit memorial was unveiled and a dawn service held, followed by breakfast, just as it was 100 years ago.

Countless people gave their time and resources to ensure the reenactment was made a reality.

I was proud to march across the pages of history in Albert's name, and form a connection to the man I never knew.

Acknowledgements

While I had my photographs as references for the illustrations, I would like to acknowledge the following for use of their images:

The Reenactment Committee, Photographer Andrew Bonnallack, Wairarapa Times Age, Wairarapa Archives, Stuff, The National Library and Limelight Theatre Company 'Once on Chunuk Bair' production photo.

The historical images are exact colourised copies of black and white photographs.

Archway for military records.

Tweet Bird, for the concept, for making it a reality and for connecting descendants with our heritage.

The Reenactment Committee and all the volunteers involved in creating a moving tribute.

As always, my family

Michelle

The Rimutaka Crossing 1915-1918
Memorial Reenactment Group

NOTES FOR THE TEACHER

Teaching points designed for years 0 – 6 as whole class activities for early primary and individual activities for middle to upper primary.

Central Idea:
The story is about the reenactment of a march that happened 100 years ago.

- Social Studies discussion points:
    How do we remember history? (Through stories, art, photos, commemorations, reenactments)
    How do you feel when you leave home for a journey? (excited? scared?)
    How do you feel when you are away on a journey? Do you miss home?
    How do you think the soldiers felt when they left New Zealand?

- Can you follow Albert's journey on a world map and see the journey he and many other New Zealand soldiers travelled during World War One?
    (New Zealand, Egypt, Suez Canal, France, England)
    Can you locate some of the countries on a world map where New Zealand soldiers fought? (Samoa (was German Samoa), Egypt, Palestine, Sinai, Gallipoli, France, Belgium)

- Numeracy:
    1,000,000 - the population in New Zealand in 1914
    100,000 soldiers went to World War On
    30,000 of these marched over the Rimutaka Ranges
    40,000 were wounded or sick
    18,000 died
    What percentage of New Zealand went to World War One?
    Can you show all of the figures above on a pie chart?
    These numbers are estimations. Can you find the actual numbers? Are they rounded up or down?

MORE NOTES FOR THE TEACHER OVER PAGE

- Visual Art, Pictorial clues:
    What kinds of illustrations are most important in this book? Why?
    Choose your favourite page? Describe the colours, expressions and detail. What can you learn from the illustrations which are not written in the book?
    What is the beginning, the middle and the end of the story?
    Can you plan a World War One book using pictures to show a beginning, middle and end?
- Literacy:
    What point of view is the story told from?
    Can you write a postcard home about the Rimutaka Reenactment? What were the main parts of your journey?

- ICT, Research:
    Did your ancestor march over the Rimutaka Crossing? Did your ancestor go to World War One?
    The 7th to 38th New Zealand Expeditionary Reinforcements marched, 1915 to 1918. Many military records are online. You can search for your ancestor at:
    www.archway.archives.govt.nz

Downloading Teacher Notes
These notes can be download from www.bms.co.nz or by contacting ms@bms.co.nz

Colour In/Complete the Picture

Teachers may copy this picture for children to colour in or complete. Questions asked can include:
What colour are the uniforms of the New Zealand Army? What was the land like around where the soldiers were marching? What was the time of the year they were marching? What was the weather like then?

Excerpt from The Crossing, copyright Michelle O'Connell

Rimutaka March Details:
The following tables illustrate the time it took and the distance marched along with the activities involved. It is estimated that each of the approximately 30,000 soldiers who made the crossing in the First World War marched 34 kilometres, making a total of about one million kilometres marched.

1915 to 1918 Rimutaka March and Journey Total distance marched: 34 kilometres					
Featherston Camp	**Rimutaka Summit**	**Kaitoke**	**Mangaroa Valley**	**Mock Battle Maymorn Camp**	**Trentham Camp**
Arrive: 0100 hrs	0715 hrs	1030 hrs	Midday	Dawn	1200 hrs
Depart: 0300 hrs	0845 hrs	--------	-------	Morning	-------
Day 1	Day 1	Day 1	Day 2	Day 3	Day 3
March	Breakfast	Bivouac overnight	Bivouac overnight	Mock Battle	Training
Times are approximate only. Marches were also made from Trentham to Featherston. From Featherston Camp, soldiers also journeyed to Wellington and then departed by ship for Egypt.					

2015 Reenacted March and Journey Total distance 23.6 kilometres						
Camp Road	**Featherston War Memorial**	**Rimutaka Hill Summit**	**Kaitoke**	**Upper Hutt War Memorial**	**Trentham**	**Wairarapa**
0300 hrs	0345 hrs	0700 hrs	1015 hrs	1115 hrs	1230 hrs	1500 hrs
0 km march	2.5 km march	12.6 km march	7.8 km march	0.7 Parade	Lunch	Home
March	March	March	March	Bus	Bus	Bus
The descendants marched from Camp Road, south of Featherston, to Kaitoke. For the rest of the journey they travelled by bus.						

More BMS Books

Enjoyed this book? The following list of books is available from BMS Books.

The Crossing by Michelle O'Connell
Leaving for the Front by Michelle O'Connell
Art I Am - Patterns of Creativity by Shona Hammond Boys
Oku Moe Moea - The dream which is bigger than I Am by Shona Hammond Boys
Always a Grunt by Mike Ledingham
Once a Grunt by Mike Ledingham
A Soldier's Life by Lou Geraets
My Life...the Meanderings of Pop Knill by Lou Geraets
The Last Newspaper in the World by Mick Stone
Autumn and Other Stories by Rotorua Writers Group
The Forgotten by Sarah Groot
Demons Inside My Mind – Life with Anorexia – Jenna Oldham

BMS is also the manager and distributor of the short film by Shona Hammond Boys:
Short Film: *Oku Moe Moea - The dream which is bigger than I Am*

LOCAL BOOKS

Local Books is a service provided by BMS to help self-published writers and other independent publishers to market their books. For more information about BMS Books and Local Books, contact:
BMS Books
5 High Street, Glenholme
Rotorua 3010
New Zealand
Email: ms@bms.co.nz and URL: www.bms.co.nz
07-349-4107
027-2096861
Int: 64-7-349 4107

www.ingramcontent.com/pod-product-compliance
Lightning Source LLC
Chambersburg PA
CBHW042003150426
43194CB00002B/112